All I Do Is Look Within

B.C. Salkind

*To all those lost souls
who look within to maybe
finally find themselves*

Author's Note

All I Do Is Look Within started with a single poem. It wasn't mean to be a whole collection. However, as I wrote, I found myself tapping into deeper parts of myself and found that I couldn't stop writing.

Over the course of my life, I have experienced so much — trauma, seeing all sorts of things, traveling, love, grief, death, and beauty. However, despite experiencing so much, there are still so many questions I have about myself and my life and the meaning of it all.

All I do Is Look Within explores this and looks within to find meaning. I hope you can find meaning or relate to at least one poem in this collection.

Comparison

When I look at you, I see everything I could be. You have everything — your lips lack the chap that mine do and your hair falls nice and neat by the wayside. Your eyes sparkle in a way mine never could.

When you write, you write the most beauty into the world — more than God above wrote into this one. You write splendid words that could make a girl just collapse.

You write about the gods above, their cruelties and their cures. All the things they've done in some Greco world that was here long before you and I. Long before you an I, I lusted for nothing. Now, however, I lust to find myself without comparison to you.

Mortal Whims

I could count the stars
While I fall to sleep
The hours before Helios
Comes back 'round again

And I could count the seconds
As time passes by
Just to make sure there's still
Seconds for me to be

And I could kiss you
A million times
To show you how much
You mean to me

But what would be the point
Control is out of my hands
Because you never belonged
To me, or mortal whims

The Final End

She took herself over the mountain where angels trod about. They closed up to hide from her view — wings furling inwards towards heart. She always wanted to believe in God though she never truly had, but in her dying hours — perhaps she finally found something none of us living ever had.

Maybe when we die and go onto our resting place, we find something — some truth — that we can't find on mortal plane. Some truth about living or some life in the future — a chance to do it again in some beautiful way before cessation — some final end — takes us away.

There They Will Remain

I have seen so much with these eyes.
So much I can talk about
Like the streets of prominent
Old cities
The way the light bounces off the pavement
On darker, rainier days
The way a waiter pours wine
The way my lover drinks it
So much
So much to see

There's so much I can't express though
Except in lyric
And rhythm and rhyme
So much that's hidden
I hide it within myself
I keep it tucked away like a talisman
In my pocket

So much about the way the light or tile looked
What the light made me feel like
Cold, alone
These sights I keep tucked in my head
And there they will remain

You Must Speak Only Kindly

I could cry
Because the way you speak
You knock yourself
Down like an earthquake
To a Greek temple
Shaking and rattling
It all about
While it tries to grasp
Its foundation to the ground
Holding on for dear life
Because once it falls
It isn't sure it will ever have time
Time to rebuild

Up and up and up
Rebuilding is hard
And may never happen
It may never be able to be saved
And certainly not replicated
For there is one you
One set of marble pillars
One frieze painted and carved
Stone-worked like that
An artist created that
An artist created you

So now you must live
You must speak only kindly
To yourself

Life to the Pages

I want to write life
Into pages unreal
I want to see their chest
Go up and down
And I want to kiss them like a lover
Tongue in mouth
Not my mouth
Heart against heart
Bare chest against bare chest
I want to create life
For this creation
Keep it real
Keep it raw
Keep it alive and breathing
For my time
And after I die

__Let Us__

Let's dance to this music
This jazzy blues
This tune up and down
Crescendo and staccato
Lets find each other in it
Like lovers under the full moon
Let's taste life like
Bitter whiskey and sweet wine
Tasting all the good and sweet parts
And the opposite too
The bitter biting parts
Let's do it together

I Love Chaos

I love chaos
I know I shouldn't
But I love the way I feel when my life
Feels like it's going to shit
When I've reached the dark night of the soul
And I'm pulled by a brick and chain
To the bottom of the Hudson
Bubbles leaving me, my lungs
They cry out for a dash of air
But I love it
I don't even know what air feels
Like in my lungs
For my suffering is eternal
Feels eternal
My chaos too
It only goes on
Like how it does in my soul

I create problems that can be solved
Because I like having the reassurance
That I can take them
Wrap them up with a nice little bow
And tuck them under the tree
I created them, so I can remove them
I bought them, so I can give them
I wish I knew how to be happy
That it wasn't so scary
Maybe if I wasn't so scared of still waters
I wouldn't have to constantly
Be swimming in deadly
For my life
My chaos feels eternal
It only goes on

Stranger

I have always been a stranger
The woman in the corner
Reading a book or the paper
While the performers perform
And the dancers dance
I have always been there
Watching, waiting
Waiting for a moment
When maybe the attention will fall on me
When someone will recognize me
Realize me
The way I long to realize myself
I am a stanger
In this world
To others, myself
And I long to be known

In You

You have always had my back
Cover my six
But always made me cover my own too
You give me kind words one moment
When those are what I need to hear
And then the next
You spit out fire

You give me what I need
What I deserve
What I feel like I deserve
Because I have always woken up
Day in and day out and eaten
Guilt and grief like breakfast cereal

I do it so often it feels like it's part of me
Like you're part of me
Even though I try to shake you
Try to remove you off my skin
Like a biting tick full of blood
But you never budge

I hear your words inside my mind
They tell me I am safe
But that I should keep watch
They tell me I am worthy
But you've never seen something so ugly
You tell me I am nothing
But without me you'd lose everything

It makes me confused
Lost
Who are you?
Why should I trust you?

I can't do this anymore
I can't live in paranoia
In fear
In you

Trauma Narrative

My doctor said catharsis could find me through rehashing horror of times past — times I shake from my head like starry little dreams, like childhood letters in the coconut tree. She says if I do this enough, create a story around it, that I will be okay again.

I want so badly to be okay — to not carry my self hatred within me like a story told to me at bedtime when I was a child. Like a talisman I hold for comfort and good luck. For my suffering has become so common, I cling to it. It has become my resting state.

I Suppose

I suppose I can be a little controlling
I like to know the times
When I need to be here or go there
I don't like when plans change

Everyone tells me I'm too uptight
That I should change
Become more okay with
Living on the fly

I don't care for the fly though
I care for the planned things
The pieces of my life
That can always be assured

I know, I guess, that nothing
Can truly be assured
I know this because
He assured me once

Told me he would never hurt me
Never leave me
Never stop showing up
But he did

I suppose I like the things
I can control
The things I know
For a fact will work out
Unlike you

College Essays

There has always been a thousand reasons
To let myself go
To disappear into the warm
Milky night of whiskey and wine
To fall deeper and deeper into easy catharsis
Easy relief
However, I take none

Not this time or the next
Instead I choose to suffer
For my suffering gives me something to
Talk about
Makes me interesting
My suffering makes me someone
Even though I am tired of suffering

How does one win in this world
When our essays of overcoming adversity
Living through trauma
Get us into college?

Feminine

I don't always feel pretty, feminine. I wear trench coats and trousers and wear my hair in a bun many days of the week. It's not that I can't style my hair into tight ringlets around my face — it's that I just won't. I have better things to do.

Perhaps that makes me less of a woman — that I spend less time on vanity and more on writing about the messiness of life. I use words — like fuck — that are not very ladylike and I talk about sex like it's no big deal; no conundrum for a woman that's had plenty.

Sometimes I will look in the mirror and think that maybe I look like a boy. That if you cut my hair down real short, you couldn't tell me from one. If I looked in the mirror and touched my face, I could see someone, anyone looking back at me on any given day.

I suppose that's the most feminine thing about me — is that I can be anyone I want. That I can go through metamorphosis, grow wings in silence, and erupt from my hiding place a new being. A creation of power.

Writers

For all those who suffer
And all those who weep
For all those who write
I give my utmost love to you
Your art
For you leave me as awestruck
As someone facing a god
In all their glory
Their natural form

I Thought About Ending it

I thought about ending it. Thought about taking my life into my hands and pulling the trigger — sending myself into some black abyss. Peaceful, quiet, dark, cool. Death might be a refuge.

I thought about it because I didn't want to be stuck on some wheel — running 'round in circles waiting for the day when I could stop running. I knew once I was on, there would be no off. There would never again be a resting state.

I thought about ending it, so I ended *it* instead. And, somehow, freed myself in the process. Now I can stop running.

Beauty in the Pursuit

I am convinced there is more to living
Than everyone will admit
There's some sort of beauty
Hidden in the indelible mess of ink
That draws its lines on us
Leaves it's mark on us
So that we will never be the same

There is beauty in the chaos
Things we can't control
That slip through our fingers
Like a thousand grains of sand
Like water in our bare hands
All the things in life escape us
And there's beauty in the pursuit

The White Letter

My grandmother wrote me a letter
Folded up nicely in
A nice, white, frilly envelope
Clad in lace and style
She wrote how sorry she was
That I had to be alone for so long
In my suffering
She'd read my poetry
And decided it was finally
Time for two people to bear the burden

I Don't Want to Die

There are days where I cry myself to sleep. Where my pillow becomes as wet as the floor after the dog drinks his water and his slobber goes everywhere. I hide within myself, looking for escape, but every corner, every doorway is stuck or blocked or impossible to open.

I don't want to die, I just want to live — safely, in peace, with some refuge where I can hide when everything in life becomes just too much.

I know I will find this refuge one day. I have to tell myself this. For I must keep living.

Poison

You are poison — sickly sweet. You coax me out to give me your putrid purple drink. I take it like my medicine and feel as it all begins to be over.

Maybe a life with you is better over though than through. For there is nothing worse than living with regrets and you are one of my biggest regrets.

I Wanted Him To Want To Be Like Me

He acted like he wasn't impressed
With everything I had done
But deep within
I think he wanted to be like me
Just as badly as I wanted to be like him

Wanted to spill out his bloody guts
Onto an inky, wet page
Covered in tears and indelible lines
That make up meaning
A part of the divine within us
That we can create
Some of us can create
Universes so small and wide

Paint strokes go across the page
The canvas
Left, right, left, right, left, right
Just as soldiers march
In cadence across the free land

He wanted to be like me
I could taste it on his lips
And maybe I wanted him to want
To want to be like me

Curse

If he could see me now, standing here as golden Athena in the Parthenon, my skin ivory and my garb golden, he would see what he'd done. Who he'd hurt with his words and tongue.

When the goddess's eyes fall upon him again. He will crumble like all of the civilizations who dare scorn her. All the toppled cities.

Stroke of Genius

I have a stroke of genius at least once a day
When my pen hits the paper and I write
All my soreness
Tenderness and pain
Into the pages of books
No one will ever see
Or even know about

The genius comes to me
Like a muse and speaks to me
Of all the pain
All the things I've seen
Without my eyes' consent
And, then, I write

Expendable Laughing Stock

They used to call me the dumb blonde because the way my golden hair bounced in its pony tail off my head. At least that's what they said. It was just a joke, funny. We should all laugh about it, haha.

I was fourteen, fifteen, sixteen already having these ideas put into my mind by friends who claimed to love me. Care about me. Value me like some golden family heirloom passed down through ten generations of ancestors. Their ghostly figures telling the next how to be.

I felt more like they valued me like some prized racehorse. Love me while I can run, but when I stop laughing, stop running, they'd rather put me out of my misery. I was just the dumb blonde after all. Expendable in the grand scheme of things.

I Am The Wind Under Your Wings

I am the wind under your wings
The rising air of hope
That pulls you forward
Up and up and up
It carries you
Graceful as a swan
Towards your innermost destination

The Resting Place of All My Regrets

Here is the final resting place of all my regrets. Here is where they sleep like faeries in flowers waiting to wake up and show me their fangs — horrific and beautiful in all their ways.

I regret not going to church even though I didn't believe in the God of my parents, for it would've been a few more moments spent with them.

I regret splishing and splashing around in deep waters, when I could've just climbed up onto the side of the pool. I regret not leaving sooner.

I regret not saying something the first time. When I knew something wasn't right — even though I was just a child. Didn't know any better. No true knowledge of wrong or right.

I regret being embarrassed when I wanted to talk about it. When I wanted to open up the whale's mouth and climb out of it like Jonah. Quit ignoring the pink elephant in the room.

I regret my silence, my complicit nature. Always going along with the wind. For it blows me like autumn leaves in the sun — golden and brown.

I regret all these things. So I will leave them here to rest. Hopefully, eternally, for there is time yet to let them wither away, no water, and die.

Chill

You are the ice on my neck
In the summer heat
Fingers dancing down my spine
You make me shiver
Cold and unfeeling
For an instant of time
A brief second
I left the sensation of your coldness
Far off in my past
Because I would rather be temperate
Than feel the chill of you again

Who am I?

I frequently ask myself
Who I am
Am I someone mysterious
In my trench coats
My cashmere sweaters
Picked up from thrift stores
Dollar bargain bins
Because I can't lay down
The cash for a new one?

Am I someone cool?
I've only smoked cigarettes
Once or twice in my whole life
Never liked the taste
Of tobacco
Reminds me of my grandmother
She lies in the earth now
As she used to lie when she was alive

Or am I someone sweet and innocent
Naive?
I wish, but I'm too jaded
And I spit hate out of my mouth
Like a spicy, green venom
Like I have something to prove
Which I do
Because sweetness doesn't get you very far
When you're seasoned
You know things
You understand life too well
You've made love to it
Too many times and now
It doesn't see the value in you anymore

I wonder if I'm one of those girls
The ones who don't think they're beautiful
But are
Their hair falls perfectly down their faces
Cascading rays of dark light
Pouring out from them
They don't see what others do
Is it possible I'm one of these?

I think it's more likely that I'm
A messy girl
My hair disheveled when the wind hits it
Not staying firm, flyaways
My lipstick smudged
I'm not cool, not mysterious
I wear my heart on my sleeve
And take drags off of cigarettes from friends
Just to be polite
Then wash it down with whiskey
Which I don't even like either

I am a mass of cells
A heart beating
Skin and hips and face and breasts
I am neither here nor there
Up nor down
I exist in some place untouchable
By aesthetic
By categorization
By knowing
I am something mystical
Like a horned beast in the woods
Majestic
Or the minotaur
I could be peaceful or hungry
Ravenous for more

For human connection
An escape from my labyrinth
An escape to see some light
Some clarity on myself
At last

You Are Simply Here

You are simply here
Simply existing
You are not lost
In some great wide world
In crashing waves
That take life
And crush it away
Eroding it into a thousand grains of sand
A long, outstretched beach of souls

You are simply living
Not in some complicated way
Knots tied together
Can't pull away
Untangle the mess
No, you are simply here

You are simply this
And all you need to do
Is simply, so simply exist

Healed

I feel healed now
Though the cuts on my arms
Leave dark scars
A memory on my body
Physical, raw, real
Reminder of the pain
I'd once succumbed to
The pit of fire
I once crawled out of

Church Tune

I search within myself
And root around
Digging through everything I carry with me
Sunglasses, the odd coin,
My wallet — cards tucked tight inside,
A random paper clip or two, a book
My memories
All of them fading and reappearing
Like ghosts in the haze
The melody of some sad tune
Played in church when I was a kid
"Amazing grace how sweet the sound"
Except no one ever saved me

I never could relate to the God of my
Mother, God of my father
Never felt drawn to it
Never felt drawn to being condemned
For a sin I never committed

I was just a kid when I was condemned
Sin I never committed
But was committed on me
I was just a kid

Now I reach within myself
The satchel in leather
I carry with me
And think of all
The things that happened to get here
I think of that church tune

Find A Way

Life will find a way
In all the desolate, dry places
Where dust storms rage
Roaring on
Plant life, foliage will grow
Green lizards, brown snakes
Will crawl and slither
Over the vastness
Of this dead earth
For sometimes the living
Comes from the dead

Mirrors and Light

I have always seen you
In the hallways
Of mirrors and light
Where rays of sun bounce along crystal
Illuminating a prism of who you are
Who I am
Looking back at myself
I am nothing extravagant
I'm average even
And my hair sits
Out of place on my head
And my figure is boyish
I am nothing quite so
Beautiful as a rose withering
Or a cherry blossom opening
A beating heart — warm and wet
I am nothing like these natural things
I am something else entirely

Open Wound

You are my open wound
The tearing of tissue and skin
The bleeding and oozing
The running of pus
Green and blood, you remind me
Always
Of all my inadequacies
All the tiny things I feel insecure about
You poke and prod
Place your finger in my wounds
And twist and twist and twist

I try to love you
Give you everything I have
I let you operate on me
Cutting me open — vivisection
You aren't gentle, but I am kind
So I let you continue

Will I Be Yours?

I have loved you in all the ways I can. Ran my hands through your hair. Kissed your lips, soft. Gazed into your eyes of ocean's edge. You, you make me. You make me alive.

You breathe into me and with all your little touches, I sing for you. My body calls out for yours. You are mine in all the ways that matter. I fear, though, that I am not yours. That you won't take me.

To Be Love

I am beautifully floating
Over coves of ocean
And mountains, outstretched hands
Towards the heavens

I am what lies between two
Lovers who sail to each other
In the night
Guided only by moonlight
And the smell of jasmine and musk
In the salty wind

To be love is to be free
To be free is to know love
For life, for others, for yourself

Reconsider

I reconsider words spoken to me
After I have slaved away
Night and day
To prove myself
And find that maybe I was enough
They were just untrue

Ruins

He whispered in my ears secret stories of places gone and dead. Wiped clean by enemy armies and crusaders — those killing mystery cults without looking at intention. Perhaps they worship good.

I had been killed before. Died like them. I had lived dead and walked out from my grave — a stoney, decaying version of who I used to be.

The temple at Eleusis stood partial, not wholly. Just as I stand partially alive after the siege, the march on myself. I am in ruins.

Clown

To be lost is to be
No questioning where you end up
For to be here is to be right
To exist is to be right

I used to exist to be right
I thought that meant I had to
Paint my face right
Paint on a big, bright smile
Wipe runny tears away
With a black tissue
My skin red with shame and guilt
But covered by concealer
Covered by the mask

How much of my life have I been masking?
I put on a happy face to pretend
I am but a clown in a freak show
An odd circus where the clowns
Are smiling, but have tears drawn on
A lost soul traveling from place to place
Stop to stop
In summer's heat
My sweat the only thing reminding
Me that I am human
And to be human is to be enough
Being lost is enough

Crow Salutation

He salutes the crows
Like he does the gods
With this tiny beady eyes
And opaline black feathers
Jutting out in all directions
Both wild and sleek
Their beaks poking out
They are just as worthy
For respect as you or me

Go Forward

I have to stop pretending
That there is some correct way to be
"Love your neighbor" as they say
So kiss whoever it is you want
Men, women, anyone else
Dance with whoever it is you want
Forget gender, class, race, socioeconomic resting
places

Don't be afraid, don't live in fear
Don't give a single fuck

They say we're supposed to be moving forward
But unless we go forward
Actually go forward
Then were just stuck here
Floating on some moving, baseless island
In the middle of the pacific
I don't want to be stuck
When there's so much great wide world out
there
If only we continue to live, progress,
Go forward

Where Beauty Rests, Where Beauty Lies

There are so many reasons to find beauty in life. So many reasons to look up to the sky and see the trees in the way, their leaves green and milky and hazing everything else above. The sky is blue and there ain't a cloud in the sky. No white puffs of air to keep the view of the atmosphere hidden. This is the perfect time for love, reflection.

It's in these simple moments you realize life is short and fickle. You could be here one second and hung out to dry the next. You could see your mother as you walk out the door and then never see her again. It's in this temporality that the beauty is found. It's in knowing this can't last forever that beauty rests. Beauty lies.

Reconnect

In some ways I have always felt isolated
Like some misfit
Stuck on an tropical island all alone
It's beauty guides me
But so does my loneliness

I long for companionship
Human touch
Human word and song
Lyric
I long to know what goes on
In everyone else's minds
Their hearts

I long for my isolation to end
I long for my prison stint to be over
I long to reconnect

Known For Something Else

I always expected I would be tall
Smart with a brain for books
Foreign languages
And beautiful
With a stunning completion
My hair nice and neat
I always expected I would be blessed
With these things at a minimum

But no, Instead I came with a
Variety of other things
Anxiety that withers me like a branch
From a sick pine tree
Highs and lows bigger than
The receding and rising of a tsunami
Depression that makes me retreat
Further and further
Into some dark and isolated cave
A single candle the only thing to guide me

I guess I always thought
I'd be more than this
More than some statistic
More than one story
My past
The things that happened to me
The things that were done
I suppose I always
Thought I'd be known for
Something else

Uncertainty

It haunts me
Every breath I take
Every decision I make
Every move
It goes with me

If I move up
It moves with me
If I move down
It follows

No matter where I dip my head
No matter where I hide in plain sight
It follows me
Uncertainty

Perspective

I have never quite known myself
Though others seem to
I am knowable to so many, but never myself
They see me and my wet, sloppy tears on my cheeks
The way my eyes turn so red and bleary
The way I hold myself in my sorrow and grief
The way I knock back shots at parties
To forget the pain
And take pills to null the ache

I have never quite been able to see my reflection in the mirror
I wear my heart of my sleeve
But am afraid that people simply see me as weak
Like being human makes me less
Even though like others know me, I know them
And I know they struggle
Cry in their rooms at home
Or scream and yell and break things
When no one is around

Questioning mortality
And how long we each have left to live
How long earth will hold and hug us
Give us breath and life and light
Before time devours us whole
Swallowing us up in one big gulp

We are all just counting down our days
Constantly looking into a mirror
And seeing our day to day
Never anything else when we want to keep it cool

Not get too serious
But look too hard and maybe we'll see it all

Unravel Me

You unravel me
Take a seam ripper and tear
Pull my stitches loose
Take me apart

I have always wanted you to know me
See every part of me
And now you can
My stuffed insides are now exposed
And my beating heart
It beats still

For you know now
Every piece of me
Every unspeakable thing
I could never say
You know it now

The Future

There's a place where you can be whoever it is you want to be. You could be a pilot and fly through golden-blue sky until reaching a destination worth reaching. Or travel the world, over oceans so blue and see things — the Eiffel Tower, cafes and baguettes. Greek temples part collapsed, part in ruin. Bull fighting and matadors.

You could be anything you want. A ghost, a spirit, some sort of sylph — invisible. Or a musician on the stage playing blaring music, the sound of jazz goes so far. Whoever it is you want to be, you can be it. In this place — the future.

It's Okay if Cigarettes Aren't Your Thing

It's okay if cigarettes aren't your thing
Or if you take drags off of them to be kind
Or drink spirits you're better off without tasting
In the pursuit of friendship

My mother used to tell me not to fall into peer pressure
Don't fall into sin
Don't put substances into your temple
Because your body is a temple
We did all sorts of exercises on abstinence
At the church where I grew up
Exercises to keep us safe
To keep us from living life
Exercises of the cross

We were told about all those who would tempt us
All those serpents and snakes
Those slithering creatures
Too free
For us, you and me
And we were told to hide from them
To shy away from them
We were told that it wasn't worth it
To get wrapped up with them
Stay away from them

These influences they could hurt you
Take parts of you and leave you only half the
Person you once were
A tube of toothpaste
And you can't put it back

Can't fit it back through the hole and into the tube
Can't keep struggling to do so
Can't keep fighting to do so
Can't return to the way it was

Or so they say
And maybe there's some truth to this
Maybe there's some truth to it alright
But maybe we are meant to be changed
For to live is to change
To be breathing is for every breath to be just slightly different
No two sentences the same
No moment the same

We are both on our way up
And on our way down
To a box in the ground
On our way to some heaven in this life
And also towards our final resting place
Deep within the wet, earthen dirt

So I suppose I shall smoke
And drink
And do whatever it takes
To make it to companionship
Whatever feels right
For we are all just on our way down
And I want to live up
Want to live un-alone
Unafraid

Sleeping Selves

At night, mind quiet
Anything seems possible
But by the light of day
Everything seems impossible

We let ourselves get bogged down by sleep
The moments just before we flow
And believe that anything can be real
These moments create us
Our dreams the very real part of us
The only part that matters

For they may never be possible
But who knows what is?
Maybe our sleeping selves
Tell us much more truth
Than the waking

Numb

Drugs make you numb
But it's easier
In my humble opinion
To be numb
Than it is to feel
Everything all at once

Grief of the Poets

I took the world in my hands
And felt the grief of all humanity
Just from being told
That they could never make it
As a writer, a poet, an artist
Any other dream worth dreaming

Their sparkling bright hope had died
Neither here nor there now
Gone as dust in the wind
Sand through my hand
Gallons of water rushing over me
Absorption, the earth

Beauty in it all
The loss and grief
The few who carry the grief
But pick up the pen anyway
When go on writing even though
There's absolutely no point
No one will ever read your work
But that's okay

As long as your words are sincere
What you put into the world
Is real and raw and authentic
Maybe someone will hear
Will see your art

Maybe someone will reach out
Like the hand of a friend
On your sad shoulder
And tap you
Let you know that you are not alone

In what you're feeling
What you write about

That even though
You are a broken, starving artist
Begging for scraps of food
Like scraps of love
Someone sees you
Relates to you

You are no longer alone
Despite what you feel

First Encounter With Hope

Milky starlight — the way her eyes looked when she looked up and finally saw a glimmer of hope. Sparkling, glittering, electrifying hope — a big ball of energy and light.

How many times had one seen it before? When her eyes were so big and so awestruck. Was this her first time seeing hope? Perhaps.

How Far You've Come

The last time I saw myself
In the mirror
My blonde hair fell just to shoulder length
My eyes were green and glittering
My mouth quivering
And a tear fell
Because for once
I was totally aware
Of just how far I'd come

My Faith Died As A Squashed Butterly

I used to have faith
Used to believe
That if I prayed hard enough
I could do whatever I wanted to
And God would forgive me

I could look up to the sky and clasp my hands
And speak some forgiveness into a world
Unforgiving

My parents dragged me to church
And I watched as people raised their hands
To music about God
When the music I loved was about
The antithesis

I have always been an outsider
A black sheep in a herd of white
A blue butterfly in a cacophony of
Orange wings
I sing a different tune
Dance a different dance
I swim against the tide
Even though I suffer for it

I have seen the faces fake and real
But the ones that are fake
The ones who wear a mask
And only pray on Sunday
Condemning others
For their unforgivable sins
Even though they themselves
Have a stick in their eye

They squash my faith like a butterfly
Wings and long legs twitching
No more flying for me
No more life for me
My faith has died

I Was Taught To Be Polite

She was all too concerned with me turning out like my grandmother when she heard I drank from the whiskey glass once or twice — always in moderation — or so I said. Though me and my friends, we threw back glass after glass.

Our crystal, clinking glasses, cheering on into the night while someone ordered round after round. Who was I to stop when she had taught me to always be polite. To self soothe when in pain. This was my self soothing.

Nothing In The Fire's Wake

I wish I knew how long it would take the rain to gather up, condense into clouds, before falling down to me. The hazy, grey light shining down onto my face. The way the light of the church used to shine on me when I was just a child.

The way the lights grew bright and hot in the bathroom where that thing happened — that dark, hot thing. Searing thing. Burning thing. It drives me crazy, the sensation on my skin. It turns me red like a little devil dressed in women's clothing and ravages my flesh. It scorches me red hot.

Oh, how I wish the rain would come. Oh, how I wish the rain would fall and stop it from searing my skin any further. Stop the red hot fire from taking me over — leaving nothing in its wake.

I Want To Be Loved

All I want is to be someone
I want to be someone so bad
That I'm willing to do whatever it takes
I'm willing to kiss whoever it is
That tells me they like my lips
Or sing to anyone
Who says they like my voice
Dance, a little ballerina, for anyone
Who wants to see me dance

I want to be loved
Because I didn't feel loved
For a very long time
I felt stabbed with a spear through the side
Bleeding out
All my love running from me
I tried to hold it in
Stop the bleeding
But I couldn't

I want to be loved
Because it makes me feel seen
I want to feel seen because
I've always been a no one
Always been a nobody

Been the girl who hides away her light
Because if someone saw it
They could dim it

I'd been dimmed before
When it rained each droplet of rain
Would come down upon my flame
And slowly, slowly, slowly

Put it out

It makes me sad
How badly I want to be seen
Want someone to know me
Acknowledge that I am me
And they are them
And we are people
Humanity
We deserve to be known

Scars and Second Chances

I ran my finger down my wrist
Touching the scar that remained
A long line of trailing skin
Hiving, bumping up
Where it had been cut

There, then, was when I had found life
In all the bad and dark places
I had found hope
A second chance

Some Ancient Whole

There is so much in this world
So much love, heartbreak
So much beauty and trauma
So much love and so much hate
How is this duality possible?

There is a mother goddess, she calls to me
A father god who sings
Of how he needs his counterpart to exist
I love this duality
This yin and yang
Sunlight and moonlight
Day and night
Cling to it like a strong, thick rope
Hung on a tree to support a swing below
I love this duality, need it

I love chaos about as much as I love peace
And I love having a story despite the trauma
I had to go through to get the story
I am a mixture of two parts
Two parts of a whole
Two parts of some ancient whole
That was around long before me

There is Beauty

There can be beauty in everything
The way she looks on a boat
In the summer afternoon
Wind through her hair
The way he smiles as he
Takes a drink from his glass
The way they hold hands
Like childhood lovers
High school sweethearts
Even though they only just met

Or in the way a lamp glows
Colorful glass
Reflecting outward with color
Reds, oranges, greens, teals
It reflects brightly and beautifully

Or even in the way a jazz tune
Sounds as it plays
The swing and bop of it all
The movement
The saxophone, trumpet, and bass

There is beauty wherever you look
So open your eyes

There Will Never Be Enough

There will never be enough days to recount everything I know about you. They way you're insecure about your hair and the way it sits when it's windy or after a long day slaving away for a better future. Something more, something greater than this. The way you feel like your biggest moments weren't brought on by you, but others who you know. All the jobs you've had, career success, aren't because of you, but because of what you've been given.

You fear you aren't enough. That your heart isn't right — that it loves wrong, beats wrong. Sings the wrong tune when everyone else is singing the same. You fear you are lost, you are lost, you are lost. You fear this.

I see the twinkle in your eyes when they talk about writing. The way it opens up that broken heart, the longing soul, and touches it. Hand reaching out to hand. Heart reaching out to heart.

You fear there is something inhuman about you, but you are more human than anyone I've ever known. You bleed red blood and are in tune with everything around you — sometimes too much so. You see the world for how it is in all it's beauty and ugliness.

Like I said, there will never be enough time to recount it all, so this is what I will leave it at. You deserve all the good things in life. Your fear is unwarranted. There is nothing bad or ugly or evil about you. You hold the multitudes within you.

<u>Bicycle</u>
I used to ride my bike
She would watch me go down that street
When I scraped my knee
Or fell over
Toppling down and down and down
Over and over again
She was always there
Watching

I wonder if she's watching now
Watching as I write these words
Like I used to write short
Made-up stories
When we pretended together
When I was just a kid

I wonder if she can see me now
Can hear these words
Knows someone remembers her

I Can Hear Them

I can hear them
Those seraphim voices
Their unknown, esoteric cries
Only for me to know
For me to hear
I can interpret them
Know them
In a way others cannot

There are few things I can do
That others cannot
But this is one
I can take life and disassemble it
Create a guide to it
Write about it
Poetry
Before reassembling it
Placing piece by piece back together
Heart now understood

It is in this way
I can understand the divine
The celestials that hear me
As I hear them
I can hear them
And I know them
Truly, deeply

You and I

You are hot like fire
You burn bright and stand out
You are known by others
Yourself
You speak like you know
Every crevice of every desert
Every canyon
Like you've run your hands over it
And felt it
You know
I want to know

I am lukewarm like water
Unsure, moveable
I am here and there
Untouchable truly
When not contained
In some box, a glass
I know nothing because
I am always changing
Shifting forms
I have no set goals
Except for to live and just be

This sets us apart
I wish I had what you had
I wish I was more fire than water

Deeply, Madly

Your love of life
Must run deep
Love deeply, madly
Love with everything you have left
To give
For otherwise you may find yourself
Not wanting to go forward

Acknowledgements

    I would like to kindly thank all my supporters throughout this writing process, although much of it was done in solitude as this collection was something that required much self reflection. *All I Do Is Look Within* truly required me to look deep within and find myself when writing.

    That being said, I would like to give a huge thanks to my fiancé, Hunter, who is a writer himself and who listened to me reading poetry for what seemed like forever. I do hope he publishes his own collection one day.

    I would also like to kindly thank the supporters of *Liminal Space*, my first poetry chapbook, because without you I wouldn't have felt inspired to write this book. So, thank you.

Made in United States
Cleveland, OH
28 March 2025